5 SIMPLE STEPS TO MANIFESTING YOUR LIFE PARTNER

JULIA STORM

How I did it in five simple steps. Trust me, if I can do it, you can!

TEXTS AND IMAGES (2016)

Find me on Instagram
@julestorm1111

For Jonathan and Baby Girl,

If I had to leave you with just one thing, it would be this: listen, my darlings, to that quiet, knowing voice within.
It's always there for you. It will keep you safe and lead you to your dreams if you let it. Quiet the world and tune your senses in to hear.

God speaks to us every day and He will show you the way.

Table of Contents

CHAPTER FOUR

FORGET EVERYTHING YOU THOUGHT YOU KNEW AND ADMIT YOU DON'T HAVE A CLUE!

CHAPTER FIVE

CLEAR YOUR BLOCKS, BLESS YOURSELF AND GET YOUR MANIFESTING PANTS ON.

CHAPTER SIX

I AM ENOUGH WITH MARISA PEER AND PLENTY OF POST-IT NOTES.

PREFACE

I was going to call this book "EUREKA, I FOUND HIM!", because I did it! I finally manifested my life partner!

After living most of my adult life single and searching, my partner Jackson and I now share a home, have a gorgeous son and a baby on the way. I get to be myself; I know I am loved and that he is wholly committed to me, our family and our future.

Honestly, it's a miracle! One I had almost given up on ever occurring.

How did I do it?
Well, that is what this book is all about.

If you are suffering, like I was, feeling that *real* love would never find you, or worse, that it doesn't even

exist, I want to share with you the exact steps I took which broke the 'curse' of my singledom.

With a lot of determination, and some wisdom from some brilliant minds, I made all my dreams come true. I found my man and we've come home to each other. I'm treated like a queen and blissfully happy in my relationship for the first time in my life. I know without a shadow of a doubt that he is my person, and I am his.

As a bonus, these steps not only totally turned my love life around, but my financial and inner life too!

I want all of this for you as well. I know you deserve it, I know you hold your head high despite that ache inside. I know your beauty, humour and how faithfully you would love if given the chance with the right person. I know how much you want to feel that love returned, stroking your cheek and making you feel safe. I know because I've been there. I had almost lost hope myself. If it can happen for me, it can definitely happen for you. You have to want it with conviction, though, and then you have to be willing to take stock, clear your blocks, open up and act on guidance. Investing in this book shows me how ready and willing you are. So buckle up, biatches.

This is what dreams are made of - *yours!*

Chapter One

No Man's Land... LITERALLY!

At 41 I was ***still*** single, still pining after the ex who broke my heart and honestly, having less than satisfying, short-lived dalliances with a variety of Mr No-way-Josés!

I couldn't understand why real love and partnership had continued to elude me.

I am attractive, smart, spiritual, well-travelled, well read and damned sexy - if I do say so myself!

I have great relationships with my family and girlfriends, but with men, it always seemed like the ones I wanted didn't want a future with me and vice versa.

I'd see women around me who were not overly attractive, were damaged, even unkind and they still had doting, committed partners and I'd envy them. I'd wonder, what do they know that I don't? What do they have that I don't?

I had left my thirties my youthful skin and optimism behind, and the saying 'Love will find you when you least expect it'" was looking like an old spinster's tale.

I really began to wonder - what the hell was going on?!

I had to admit two things: (1) the common denominator was me and (2) I may just be one of those people who wasn't designed for coupledom. I may *not* be destined to find my 'one' in this life.

The first rang true. The second was like a punch in the gut, and I absolutely refused to believe it! My heart, soul, body and mind *knew* love was my destiny!

"Enough!" I thought.
"Even if it *is* true, before I throw in the towel, I'm going to make **one last wholehearted effort** to draw my soulmate into my life, and if it doesn't work, I'll let the quest go!"

I decided then and there that I was going to *fully focus*, call on all the powers of the universe at my disposal and be absolutely *proactive* in a way I'd never been before.

I was going to actively harness my own personal ***power*** and the ***power*** of the universe to bring my life partner to me.

"Help me Lord, show me the way." I prayed.

Chapter Two

Intention, Clarity and Letting Go

First, I needed to figure out precisely what I was looking for - or else, how was I going to find it?

Ultimately, I think we all want the same thing:

Real, soul shaking, life making, no-need-to-be- faking love!

What that looks like though will be different for all of us.

Are you willing to think outside the box in your quest to bring true love into your life?

Without serious intention and commitment to your own cause, this isn't going to work, but I know that if you were drawn to buying this book you must be *wholeheartedly* ready, willing and able.

First things first, get really clear on what your ideal relationship looks like.

You think you already know? I challenge you to answer the following questions without surprising yourself.

Approach these questions as though he or she will be made from the clay of your answers. Be honest with yourself; there's no wrong answer, only what's right for you. Writing the answers will magnify the power of your energetic intention. Grab your pen and paper, and let's doo dis!

* What does your ideal mate look like?

*What do they earn?
*How old are they?
* What is their passion?

* How do they show up for you?

* Where do they live?

* Do they have kids?

* What do you do together?

* Is he or she sporty?

* Level of education?

* What career are they in?

*How long after you meet until you kiss?

* Sleep together?

* Do you move in together?

* When do you get engaged?

* Get married?

* Will you have children, if so when, how many?

* What does the relationship bring you that you can't get on your own?

Now answer this: do any of the people you've been dating or pining after remotely resemble this person?

If you are anything like me, this exercise will show you exactly how you waste your time and energy with people that are *so* not suited to you - unfair for both you and your soulmate.

I'll tell you a story about the one I couldn't let go of. My miracle occurred when I finally did.

My spiritual home is Hamilton Island: a beautiful island resort in the Whitsundays, Queensland, Australia.

The story as to why I consider it my spiritual home is for another book, but needless to say, I love this island with a love akin to a best friend, and I truly feel this island loves me the same. I feel her calling me back when I'm not there, though a part of me is always with her.

Do you have a spiritual home? Do you have that same special feeling for a particular place unlike any other? Let me know on my Facebook page. I'd love to see photos. I'll show you mine - I have pictures of my island up all over my house. I put them up after my parents passed away. I couldn't get to my island to heal so I brought her energy into my home, and looking at them every day helps me maintain my home energetically as my happy place.

I digress.

So it was that in the year 2006 I was living and working on Hamilton Island, having again - for it was my fourth time as an employee of Hamilton Island Enterprises - the absolute time of my life.

I'd formed some great friendships, and our lives revolved around working, partying and enjoying all

that the Great Barrier Reef had to offer:
jet skiing, snorkelling, drinking, swimming, day trips to the reef, to other islands; more drinking and dancing into dawn at the small nightclub on the island itself.

So few guests went to the nightclub that it seemed like a nightly private party for staff members, all of whom were in their twenties; sun-kissed, a little bit wild and living the dream.

We drank *a lot* of alcohol, and there were new flirtations amongst staff members weekly - even nightly. Very few serious relationships were formed amongst these shenanigans.

Around my seventh month of living back on the island, I organised a week off to go home and see my family. My mum and I co-owned a house on the Gold Coast, and I was looking forward to seeing her, my sister and my niece. I also wanted to catch up with my old friends and detox a bit from the hyper, hectic social life I was leading on Hammo.

Mum had mentioned in passing that a couple of young guys had moved into our complex, across from our house. I thought nothing of it, consumed as I was with my crush of the week on the island.

I loved being back home with my family. I could, for the first time in months, truly be myself and relax; something I had yet to master out in the world.

I vividly remember the moment I saw Greg. It's a moment that's forever cast under its own spotlight in my mind, and that's exactly how it felt at the time. Cue the heavens opening:

beams of light streaming down,

angelic choir sounds,
Time s...l...o...w...i...n...g...

And there he was.

Blonde curls above a pretty boy face and eight pack abs. What was not to love?!

To me, he *literally* had the face of an angel, and as ridiculous as that sounds and as I feel admitting that, he really was my idea of what the perfect guy would look like.

He was *sooo* friggin' hot!

Though we were introduced, disappointingly nothing of note happened between us that first visit, and by the time I was back on the island and in party mode, he pushed to the back of my mind – that is,

until a few months later, when I was ready to resign my job and leave Hamilton.

Having worked extensively at some of the Australia's most stunning resorts, and multiple times on my favourite, Hamilton Island, the hospitality industry was one that I loved and enjoyed; regardless of how beautiful the locations were, how much fun I had with the customers and the lifestyle, there would

always come a time when paradise lost its energetic hold and I'd have to move on.

That time had come by March 2007.

Though I hadn't thought of Greg prior to deciding to leave, once the decision was made and I was approaching my final week on the island, a profound, almost other-worldly (cue that heavenly choir again) *knowing* came over me. I *knew* that when I returned, Greg and I would be together.

Within a few weeks of landing back on the Gold Coast, we were.

Never have I felt anything like the magnetism and obsession that I felt for Greg. When he was loving towards me, I felt complete joy and self-acceptance, and so much love; so much happiness. I really thought I'd found my 'One'. I couldn't fathom us not being together forever, this feeling was so profound. I truly believed we were soulmates.

However, when he turned cold - as he seemed to increasingly do after the first few blissful months - it was a physical wretched pain, one that robbed me of any self-esteem and filled me with the panicked terror that he would leave me.

We were not well suited. I was 10 years older than him, and ready to get married and have his babies – immediately - in the throes of the overwhelming love I felt for him. Any and all urges to party left behind, I just wanted him and our family life to begin.

He, on the other hand, was at a totally different place in his life - still heavily into partying and trying to make his mark on the world. Definitely not ready for marriage and babies, and more than a little overwhelmed by just how I was into him. I remember him telling me, "No-one has ever liked me this much."

In retrospect, I can see that I had completely lost my mind. Myself. His love was a drug and I was addicted. When he withdrew affection, I suffered actual physical withdrawal symptoms and fought feverishly to get my next hit. Twisted myself into a pretzel and negated my own needs to please him.

Of course, I was destined to fail. Selling yourself out for another is unsustainable. Energetically, you will hit a wall or the other person will lose all respect for you and leave you. Both seemed to happen simultaneously for us.

I couldn't jump when he told me to jump. It was now as painful to be in the relationship as it was to imagine being without him.

He was no longer committed nor faithful to me, and I had burnt myself out in fighting for his love.

Like with children who become spoilt when given too much too easily, Greg became cruel, enjoying wielding his power over me and seeing how he could hurt me. When he finally left me, I welcomed it,

though it broke my heart into a million pieces and it brought me an overwhelming pain – only surpassed years later by the death of my parents.

It was losing Greg that brought me back home to myself.

Excruciatingly at first.

Initially, I was a broken-hearted shell of a person. I pined after him with a constant ache.

To heal I had to grow. I had to dig so deep to find something in myself to hold onto during that time. I felt so empty, unloved, rejected and insecure. All my mojo had evaporated, or was still wrapped around Greg's leg, begging to be filled back up.

Brick by slow, heavy, aching brick, I rebuilt myself in love, true self-acceptance and absolute fortitude.

I had to, in order to function and survive.

It's a foundation that is solid and unshakable now, independent of the opinions of others or the changing winds of circumstance. It took *seven years* - seven years people! - during which I would still reach out to Greg every half year or so.

For a long time, a part of me still hoped my absence would make him realise that we *were* meant to be together. I believe in some ways he did realise what we had was special, but we were and are two puzzle pieces that don't quite fit. In retrospect, his reticence

and withholding have been blessings that forced me to find value in myself in the face of incomprehensible painful rejection.

Today, I am only grateful for the experience. I know I couldn't love and value myself as I do without that experience with Greg.

I also choose only to remember the love - that great big beautiful feeling - and while I no longer feel the same way I did for Greg, he will always be very special to me, as he really was an amazing soul who changed my life.

More often than not, letting an illusionary love go is a painful experience; if the other person reciprocates a lot less and you have to supress many aspects of yourself, please know that this is a false love. But it's through this experience that I was able to go on to create real love and knew unequivocally when I had found it.

Chapter Three

Making Space for Love

In declaring my intention, I researched Feng Shui, designed specifically to draw love in. I'm sure you are well aware that Feng Shui is the Chinese art of creating harmonious surroundings to balance yin and yang energy.

A home has certain energy spots that pertain to different aspects of our lives, e.g. financial, familial

and romantic. Certain arrangements of furniture, décor and natural elements such as colour, water and wood can unblock these energy centres and are said to assist in manifesting positive outcomes in these areas of our lives.

Whether you believe in it or not isn't as important, in my opinion, as having the commitment to use all the resources at your disposal. This includes the metaphysical, in *affirming* your *intention,* and willingness to *embody* your *desire* to bring love forth to you. In other words, showing the universe you are willing to do whatever it takes to create the relationship of your dreams. I did this as a part of my quest, so I'm passing it on to you. What have you got to lose?

In line with this, I made literal space in my home for a man. I replaced my couch with one that a couple could more easily snuggle on. I changed my decor from very feminine, to a style that a man could feel equally at home in. I tried seeing my home through the lens of the relationship I wanted, and adjusted in preparation. I went so far as to buy myself engagement cards. Like I said, I was holding nothing back and I refused to allow the fear of appearing foolish to stop me.

Various websites have different tips for how to use Feng Shui to attract love. I placed red coloured items and books on soulmates and love in the right-hand corner of my bedroom next to my bed. I removed

photos of my son and parents from the bedroom and - please don't think it's necessary for you to do the same – even purchased a new, bigger bed and fresh bed linen that had "His" and "Hers" embroidered on the pillow.

I vowed to myself that I'd only allow the person who I seriously thought could be my life partner to sleep on the "His" pillow.

When my son's father was the first male to lay upon that pillow, I was worried that I had screwed up the intention power of my Feng Shui. We were not together, not in love and he was definitely *not* going to be my life partner.

I discovered much later that the joke was on me.

Chapter Four

Forget everything you thought you knew and admit you don't have a clue

Honestly, if you knew anything about the opposite sex, you would have someone romancing the pants off you, adoring you and planning their future with you right this very instance. Sorry, I know that's harsh, but coming to that realisation about myself was life changing.

I thought I understood men. I'm interested in psychology and human behaviour, and had read extensively on both subjects. I thought that if I looked good, was hot in bed and pandered to a man's

ego, I'd get the adoration I craved. I was wrong. So wrong. Like Jon Snow, I knew nothing.
Thank the universe that I came across the work of Alison Armstrong at that time. Alison coined the phrase 'frog farmer', a term describing a woman who, rather than turn a frog into a prince, turns a prince into a frog. I could completely relate.

Reading Alison's books and then doing her online course, *The Queen's Code*, not only opened my eyes to my mistaken beliefs about men and the resultant non-conducive behavioural choices I made with them, but healed a lifetime of built up fear and resentment that had accrued through that misunderstanding and the actions of a few unhealthy men.

Alison also teaches men how to better understand women, and I truly believe her life's work of helping us understand that the opposite sex is vital for the transformation of humanity, and healing the pain of patriarchy for both sexes.

Through my learnings from the course, I softened, became more open and trusting with the men around me; willing to let them help me, support me, show me their goodness. It was obvious that until then I had been entrenched in my own masculine defensive energy without realising it.

From the outside, I had always looked like a real girly girl, but I was tougher on the men in my life than I ever was on my women friends. I unwittingly pushed them away, and then blamed them for

leaving.

My father had not been a safe person for me, and therefore despite my best intentions to heal from my past, all men had been tarred by the brush of my mistrust.

Sound familiar?

Such as it is, there's no sense beating yourself up about it. Simply empower yourself with knowledge, allow the misunderstanding to be corrected, and let those who have spent their lives dedicated to researching the things you and I don't fully comprehend impart the wisdom they've acquired.

As a result of my shift, men began responding differently to me. They seemed eager to help me, in any innocent way. My son's father, strangers, male acquaintances, all started going out of their way to provide for me, emotionally and physically. I began to be treated like a queen for the first time in my life.

An example of what now continues to be a regular occurrence was a small encounter at a bottle shop. An older man, standing in line behind me, offered to carry the case of Coronas I'd just bought to the car for me. My former self would have declined his offer, thinking there must be a perverse hidden agenda.

Thanks to Alison's books and course, I now saw men differently; saw and respected their noble desire to provide for and protect women. I was therefore able to graciously accept his offer.

The kind sir and I talked about his wife and family on the short trip to the car, and he was definitely not creepy - but a complete gentleman. Seeing his chest swell with joy simply because of my sincere thanks was heart-warming. I wished I had read Alison's work in my twenties.

"The more you learn about men and their world and why they do what they do, the more naturally receptive to them: you will just be, effortlessly. And as you find out how willing and able they are to give you what you need most, you'll relax and be able to accept them." Excerpt from 'Making Sense of Men, A Woman's Guide to a Lifetime of Love, Care and Attention from All Men' Alison A. Armstrong

As I said, her work includes guidance for men on how to decipher the women in their lives, if you're a man reading this. Check out the free audios on her website, www.understandmen.com. Her work is the most comprehensive I've encountered on the subject, and filled in the blanks that my previous readings had missed.

Just as a proviso, there is a difference between a healthy and an unhealthy man. You will never be treated like a queen by an unhealthy person. Alison's work helps you determine what constitutes the noticeable differences between a healthy and unhealthy man - something a great many women have difficulty discerning due to their care-taking, compassionate natures.

I have to admit, I thought of applying this new learning to winning my ex back, but during this time my relationship with my son's father, Jackson, began to develop.

Friends and co-parents, we had never been in love with each other. We had still been getting to know each other better when I discovered I was pregnant.

My son is my gift from God, as his name, Jonathan, denotes. There was absolutely no doubt in my mind that I would have my baby and I thank God every day for my most precious son. He is truly the best thing that has ever happened to me.

On learning I was pregnant, I realised that I very much doubted Jackson and I would still be seeing each other by the time our child was born.

Nor were we - and the joy I felt in becoming a mother was tinged with pain for my son, believing that he may not have his father in his life. I did everything in my power to forge a strong connection with Jacko so that we would still be family, though we weren't a couple.

It was a hard-fought battle. Our friendship was tenuous and volatile in the early days, as Jackson's wild ways gave me cause to distance him at times. Later, as he slowly became more involved with us, it wouldn't be uncommon for me to rage and criticise him when the negative behaviours and risky choices he was making threatened to impact his ability to be there for Jonathan in a positive way.

I was fighting for my son so that he could have a loving, healthy relationship with his dad.

To Jackson's credit, regardless of what else was going on in his life - and despite also having the single most traumatic childhood of anyone I've ever met - he has always been there his children, and valued them above everything. For many years however, he had a foot in two worlds that were completely incompatible.

My own life completely revolved around raising my son, especially in those early years. There was absolutely no prospect of romance in my life, nor interest in it on my part, so occasionally Jackson and I would find ourselves in bed together simply due to proximity and opportunity.

I had no romantic interest in him – I was purely scratching an itch. I was always able to be myself with him, and there was no emotional fallout from being intimate with each other. Not for a long time, anyway.

I completed Alison's course the year my son started school and Jackson, having also made steps to grow and change, was pleasantly surprised by the softness he'd never seen in me before, and began responding with his best self. A self that, in all honesty, I had doubted existed in him. He became romantic, gentlemanly, reliable and considerate.

One night, we found ourselves in bed together and it

was... different. There was a gentleness and an intimacy to it. It might seem odd, but I had never once considered him to be the love that I was looking for. The water under our bridge was murky and choppy, definitely not the lapping silken sea of my dream relationship. It wasn't long before we had a big blow up and retreated to the friend zone again.

Most people don't realise that it is their unconscious limiting beliefs about love, relationships, the opposite sex and even money that keep these things away. Alison held a mirror to mine and started me on the path to remodelling my belief system to match my heart's desires. Do you have any unconscious beliefs that could be blocking you from creating the love you've always dreamed of? You can test yourself by answering the following questions honestly:

* Do you trust men? If you're interested in women, do you trust them?

* Do you emasculate the men in your life? Do you objectify the women in your life?

* Do you repress yourself in the presence of the opposite sex? Or in the presence of your own gender?

Write down the first three things that come to mind when I ask you:

* Love is...?

* Men are...?

* Relationships are...?

One of my old beliefs still popped up just then as I was typing. The word 'work' whispered in my brain as the answer to the last three questions. Thankfully, I now have the tools to clear and delete that belief, as I'll describe in the next chapter. The fact that a whisper of it still exists after the enormous amount of diligence and effort I have put into clearing my limiting beliefs, the ones that don't serve me, shows the absolute power that they hold over us and why they often become self-fulfilling prophecies if not addressed.

If you are more inclined to the scientific over the metaphysical, Alison Armstrong and her extensive research and experience will go a long way in helping you shift your erroneous beliefs about the gender differences.

Alison Armstrong, Author

www.understandmen.com
www.queenscode.com

Chapter Five

Clear your blocks, bless yourself and get your manifesting pants on

I like to listen to a lot of personal development webinars. I'm always looking for assistance in actualising myself.

I came across the work of Christie Marie Sheldon through my subscription to Mindvalley Academy, a web-based school featuring a variety of experts in the Personal Transformation field.

Christie is an energetic healer, whose work is based around helping people raise their energetic vibration to that of 'love' or above. The theory is that emotional states can be energetically calibrated to a vibrational frequency, with the lower states being sadness and apathy, moving slightly higher with anger; and the highest states love, joy and gratitude.

Not only does it feel better to vibrate at higher emotional frequencies, but those who believe in the Law of Attraction maintain that we draw to ourselves experiences mirroring the energy we are embodying. Therefore, manifesting at the highest vibrational frequencies rather than the lowest obviously brings you more of what you want - not what you don't want.

I decided to do Christies 'Love and Above' course online through Mindvalley Academy, and was so impressed I went on to do her 'Unlimited Abundance' course.

There may be some who think the concepts behind Christies work are too 'out there', or not based in reality, but I can honestly say, of all the steps I list in this book and the experts who have helped me, Christie's courses impacted me the most.

Within a few short months of completing both courses, I went from being an unemployed single mother with a dismal romantic life, struggling to make ends meet, to happily living with my life partner, employed, working with fantastic people less than five minutes from my home. I created the relationship I'd always wanted and doubled my income, and I truly believe Christie's work was a primary influencer in that occurring for me.

The job that I landed in was the one I'd worked at for three years until the birth of my son. The strange thing was that I had asked for my job back, once my son was a little older, only to be told there wasn't a position for me - and through the rumour mill, the implication was I wasn't welcome back.

At that time, I was deeply hurt and confused as my former manager, Socky, and I were still close. It had been the best working environment I'd ever experienced. I chalked it up to higher management resenting me for leaving, but honestly, I had no clue as to the real reason.

So when I began to apply for jobs and messaged Socky to ask if he would provide me references, I was shocked and thrilled when he offered me my job back.

The clearing of my personal blocks and erroneous beliefs through Christie's course opened the door for this miracle, and the miracle of drawing my life partner to occur.

There were a number of beliefs I had to clear that I didn't realise were blocking my manifestations.

This included: *men don't know how to love well

*love is work

* people just end up hurting/disappointing you

*money causes conflict

* people deep down don't like me

One of the most deep seeded and harmful beliefs I held unconsciously was that because God had already gifted me with my beautiful son, if I asked for more, in the form of a life partner or abundance, God would punish my greed by taking my son from me.

You can imagine how shocked and horrified I was to find that buried nugget in my psyche. I wept for myself. Wept that a part of me truly felt that way, so scared and mistrusting that goodness in all forms could be mine, and wept that I may have been heretofore sabotaging myself in love due to the terror of that hidden belief.

Clearing, deleting and blessings became my mantras. For a month solid I diligently addressed every

harmful thought and layer upon layer there was. A lifetime of painful, frightened, hurtful messages received that I'd held onto.

I'd clear one, and another equally awful, distorted thought would pop into my mind - so I'd delete that and then the space between limiting beliefs and thoughts became wider and wider until after that month, I was left with a predominately quiet, peaceful mind and a relaxed, joyous disposition.

It just makes sense that one would create grander things from joy and ease, than from an energy of mistrust and fear.

Exercise

When you catch yourself thinking a negative thought or holding a limiting belief, simply say to yourself in your mind: 'I clear, delete, uncreate and destroy the belief that _____ across all time, space, reality and dimensions.'

To raise your vibration instantly use the mantra: ' I bless _____ with pure love and light, I bless _____ with pure source energy.'

Seems simple enough, doesn't it? Too easy almost? Its power is in applying it to **all** the blocking thoughts. Not just doing it for a day, but *really* catching yourself in the moments when your mind has led you down a scary path and your energy is sending hazardous signals to the universe. Noticing

when you are hardening your heart, or raising the emotional wall and sinking into negativity; when you're feeling like there is not enough and especially when you are telling yourself that something about you yourself is unlovable, unworthy or wrong. Those are the moments that undone will not only set you free but speed your love to you on the beams of light that have broken through your darkest thoughts.

www.ChristieSheldon.com/GIFT
www.ChristieSheldon.com/Wealth Consciousness

Chapter Six

I am enough with Marisa Peer and plenty of post- it notes

Braithe, the 10-year-old who lived next door, peered at the little post-it note stuck on the foyer mirror.

"I am enough," he read aloud slowly.
He then looked at me quizzically.
"Why have you got all these stuck everywhere?"

I had anticipated hearing that question over and over when I stuck little yellow post-its bearing the words 'I AM ENOUGH' on almost every visible surface of the house the night before. Mirrors, cupboards, doors and walls, everywhere you turned, you would see a post-it note that said the same thing: 'I AM ENOUGH'.

"Well Braithe," I said, "these notes are meant to make anyone who reads them feel really good about themselves.". Until it came out of my mouth, I hadn't really known how I was going to explain the little love letters adorning my house. I internally high- fived myself. That will work, I thought.

With a typical child's acceptance, he shrugged his shoulders, gave me a 'you're-weird-but-ok' look, and went off to find my son Jonathan.

I had also set a daily reminder alert on my phone. I'm still alerted to the reminder that 'I AM ENOUGH' everyday, though the post-its have long since fallen.

Marisa Peers, a world-renowned hypnotherapist, says that in her professional opinion, as a leader in her field who works with celebrities, politicians and elite athletes as well as teaching and reaching thousands of people via Mindvalley Academy, the basis of all human suffering is the feeling and perception that we are somehow not enough as we are.

It was after listening to a webinar of hers in which she instructed a very famous, successful and desperately unhappy client to place the post-it note messages to himself around his mansion that I decided to do the same. If it's good enough for Mr Rich-and-Famous, it's good enough for me, I thought. Besides, what, other than a few awkward looks or questions from visitors, did I have to lose? What do you?

I truly believe this was a subtle, yet vital part of shifting my energy to be able to receive what I've always dreamed of.

Over the weeks that the notes were on display, they received a lot of attention from the myriad of visitors - adults and children alike - who came to the house. Their reactions were almost always the same. When I explained the intention behind the notes, it was nonchalantly acknowledged – and then we'd move straight on to the next topic.

I did notice, though, that spines straightened and smiles widened after they read the little post-its. Unconsciously, the message was getting through.

A solid, centred feeling within me became more and more my norm. I was much more accepting of myself, less critical of my appearance and less inclined to force myself to do things that I didn't want to do simply to please others.

Such a subtle, simple tool, but it's a gift I still give myself every day. I remind myself that *I am enough*. Self-love is literally the foundation for all expressions of love, giving and receiving, and the most powerful energetic vibration to manifest your life partner from. It can't be faked, and it has nothing to do with looks or accomplishments.

If you've been playing along and following the steps, your foundations should feel solidified, debris and blocks removed and the space without and within you rearranged to make room for your soulmate. Can

you feel your mind and heart opened? If so, we are now prepared for the final step. This preparation is so important, because once all the internal puzzle pieces are properly placed, it's as though a cork is popped; and the manifestations of not just romance and love, but of abundance and opportunity that have previously been dammed will flow from you like a river that's broken its bounds. It's then up to you to grab the reins and take inspired action as these opportunities arise - led by that quiet, knowing voice within.

Chapter Seven

Intuition and Inspired Action

Let your guts, not your head, heart or loins, lead you to him

The universe wants you to find him, to live your dream love. It's been talking to you about it the whole time. Sometimes the timing isn't right. Sometimes you need to grow to be able to receive big love.

I'll give you a few examples of following your inner guidance to find him.

A dear friend of mine was involved with a man who did love her dearly, but just couldn't commit. He couldn't even commit to dinner, let alone to a real future. Every time she had had enough and broke it off with him, she would go onto a dating website. A series of disastrous dates would follow, and she would find herself back with Mr Noncommittal. She was between a rock and a hard place.

One day she came to me and told me she felt it was time to move back down south, where her closest relatives lived. She wanted to get away from the stressful relationship she was in and be nearer her family for the first time since she had left her home state, ten years previously.

As much as I knew I would miss her, I also felt this was exactly what she needed to do for herself. I had a real sense that she would find her 'person' with her family. Her choice to move was coming from the best part of her, the authentic, heart-centred part, and when we make choices from the bravest, boldest, best in ourselves - ***magic happens***.

She met her fiancé online a few months after her move.

She was never destined to meet him up north, where I live. She also wouldn't have met him if she was still embroiled in the self-esteem damaging cat-and- mouse game Mr Noncommittal was playing.

We need to rise to meet our future, be quiet enough inside to hear the guidance, and then be courageous enough to act.

Here's another example.

"I'm getting off Tinder," Nikki declared.

We were having coffee in my backyard on one of those perfectly temperate sun-steamy mornings that the Gold Coast is known for.

Having left her long-term relationship half a year earlier, Nikki was struggling in the dating world. An absolute head turner with a wicked sense of humour and a great sense of style, she tended to go for the bad boys and inevitably ended up frustrated and unhappy.

Online dating wasn't proving any more fruitful for her, either.

"This guy just messaged me from Tinder. He looks good, but I'm just over the whole thing." She sighed.

"I can imagine," I commiserated. "Show me who messaged you, babe."
"I haven't even replied, I think I'll just delete my Tinder account now."

She pulled out her phone, tapped at the screen, and handed it to me. The good looking young guy in the photo looked so familiar, yet I couldn't place him. I told her as such.

"Who is he? Where does he live? I asked

From what Nikki shared, I realised I didn't actually know him - yet the feeling that I did was unusually strong.

"You know babe," I said to Nikki, "sometimes a feeling of familiarity is the universe's way of tapping you on the shoulder, saying 'hey, this person has a message for you' or that you've known them in a past life, or that you're *meant* to know them in this one. I think you should message this guy before you delete your account."

It didn't take more than that to twist her arm. She must've felt drawn to him energetically to have brought him up in conversation in the first place. I also knew this was about her, not me, though I was the one feeling the familiar feeling.

Her life changed with that first message.

They now live together in his home town, a few hundred kilometres north of the Gold Coast. They bought a great big slobbering dog together, are planning their future, and this is the happiest and easiest relationship Nikki has ever been in. He is her person, she is his. That little inner prompt to show me his photo gave her the boost she needed to reach out, just when she was ready to give up.

Example numero three.

I met Sylvia through Jackson. She was the girlfriend of one of his best friends, Tony. They lived right around the corner, and one time, when Jackson was living with me, he invited them both over for a few drinks.

I wasn't the biggest fan of Tony's. While a good guy

deep down, his raging alcoholism made him difficult to be around. Jackson was one of the few who could keep him in line, but also knew that if it got out of hand, it would be up to him to get Tony to leave.

Sylvia was a vibrant Brazilian with long flowing brown hair, that famous Brazilian bikini bod and a wide smile. I liked her the moment I met her. She had a naturalness and authenticity that puts you straight at ease. I often wondered what the hell she saw in Tony, to be honest.

We became firm friends after that first meeting, and as we lived so close to each other would catch up regularly for a chat.

One morning, I received a phone call from Sylvia. She was distressed - Tony had kicked her out of their home in one of his drunken rages. She'd spent the night on the couch of a friend, but was wondering if she could stay in the spare room at my house, since Jacko had recently vacated.

I knew it wouldn't be a long term arrangement but I welcomed the opportunity to have Sylvia as my flatmate.

We spent many nights musing over our relationship mistakes. Sylvia still loved Tony despite his many faults. She felt she hadn't truly been herself in the relationship, going along too much with what he wanted to do then resenting him for it.

"I feeel I neeed to geeve 'eem one more shance," she told me in her gorgeous Portuguese accent. She was desperately hoping her absence had made him realise that what they had was for treasuring, not sabotaging. He was ringing and messaging her every day to come home, and after a month at mine, she was ready to give it another go.

Of course, Tony was on his best behaviour for a while. I know he loved Sylvia - to be honest, I know he loves her still, but his alcoholism and the underlying issues that caused it were destructive bedfellows, and within a few months another episode occurred, with Tony again kicking Sylvia out of their home. Heartbroken, Sylvia knew there was no going back this time.

Meanwhile, on the other side of town, Louie had just secured the ultimate bachelor pad. Stunning water views, a pool, spa and sauna and the best part? It was situated in the building above The Grand Hotel, our local watering hole. Louie had recently become a fixture at The Grand since his partner of 16 years had ended their relationship, just six months before. He had to move out of the family home - next door to mine – which they'd lived in with their two school- aged sons.

Louie had been a broken man. Depressed and missing seeing his sons every day, he spent many days lamenting to me the loss of his family and many nights drowning his sorrows at The Grand. Deciding to rent above the pub was his way of pulling himself out of his funk and embracing the change that had occurred.

"You know you'll meet someone now that you have the ultimate bachelor pad," I teased him.

"Not me," he countered "I just want to have fun now, definitely not up for anything serious."

Famous last words. That first weekend of officially moving into his bachelor pad, newly-single Sylvia and I were out for a few drinks and ran into Louie at The Grand. Introducing them to each other, the air crackled with electric attraction.

They've not been apart since that night - I attended their beautiful beach wedding just recently.

They are both happier than they have ever been in their lives. I love that I played a small role in helping these two find each other, and I would love to play a role in helping you, too.

Don't worry, you won't necessarily have to move states or be dumped and get your heart broken to be led to your person. You *will* have to be able to listen to your intuition, your heart and the inner knowing voice. You *will* have to be brave. You will also have to get out of your own way and let the universe lead you to him.

How often do you follow your hunches? Do you ignore nudges, only to slap your forehead later realising you knew this or that would happen, but you'd let your mind dissuade you from following your gut?

When I started to get serious about letting spirits guide my choices implicitly, I would ask for guidance on everything: which directions to take whilst driving, which books to read or buy, social engagements to say yes or no to and purchases to make or pass on.

Often, I would find myself driving and get that familiar tap in the centre of my chest, followed by either words or a picture or just a sense of what I should do.

Each time I've ignored it, I felt icky immediately - and lo and behold, something I would've preferred to avoid came to pass. Every time I've followed it, I've been rewarded.

Later, when you live each day like this, you aren't always going to immediately see what the benefit of following the hunch was, but by then your trust in the guidance will be so unshakable that you know unequivocally there was one.

To strengthen your ability to tune into your own higher self's inner guidance, Christie Marie Sheldon has a wonderful exercise called 'The Closet of Yes and No'.

Exercise

Picture yourself standing in front of a walk-in

wardrobe filled with clothes, but divided into two parts. On the left hang your 'YES' clothes, and on the right your 'NO' clothes.

Picking from the YES clothes, put an outfit on in your mind's eye.

What colours are you wearing? What materials are the clothes made of? Are they long or short? Loose or tight? Do you have accessories on? Shoes?

Now with your gorgeous YES outfit on, really feel into what your YES
feels like to you.

What feelings does it generate in your body? Where in your body can you feel your YES?

When you've really come to know what a wholehearted YES feels like for you, imagine removing that outfit, putting it back in your wardrobe, turning to the right and choosing your NO outfit.

Put it on and again, what colour are the clothes? Style?
Fit?

Length?

Material?

How does it feel to wear your NO?

Where in your body does a firm, unshakeable NO live?

How does NO feel?

Do you see how differently your YES and NO feel within you?

Now tell yourself something that you know is true, like 'My name is (insert your real name).'. Do it again putting a different name in. Again, can you feel the difference within you? Not in your mind, but within your body? The body is where your true knowing resides.

I question all my decisions in this way. I ask or say, 'It is in my best interests to do this.'. Then feel if that statement feels like my 'Yes' or my 'No'.

It's one of the reasons I've been able to successfully traverse some of the rocky relationship terrain with my partner. Even when sometimes my human mind is frustrated with him, my inner self knows we are meant to be together.

I debated putting this in the book. The reality that, even when you find your soulmate, it's not always

going to be a bed of frangipanis. I want you all to feel positive and inspired and open to love. I just thought it important to emphasise that the connection to your intuition will not only bring you both together but will help in keeping you connected.

Let's face it, if you've been single as long as I was, you aren't going to be perfect partner material. It's a learning curve and definitely has been a steep one for me. I'm not used to relying on a man, trusting a man, sharing or being accountable to a partner.

I love who I'm becoming and I truly believe manifesting my partner and feeling at peace with that aspect of my life has opened the door for my soul's other purposes, my creativity, to finally be birthed. As it has been in writing this book, with an ease and joy I would only ever dreamed of in the past.

My dreams for myself had always consisted of meeting my soulmate, becoming a mother and writing my book. Seemingly impossible for me to achieve for so many years, similar to the hopelessness I felt in love, I truly thought I would never actually be a writer. I had begun to believe I couldn't write, had no talent or ability, that I was just an avid reader who appreciated writing. I am so glad I was wrong about myself and that one of the most amazing gifts of manifesting my life partner, is the way it has affected my sense of self and actualisation of other lifelong dreams. With one came the other. I wish this and so much more for you.

"He's here."

I heard the voice clearly as I sat in the backyard with my good girlfriend and my son's father, lamenting over the most recent disappointment from the man I was currently seeing.

They were helping me formulate my text messages to this guy, and were pretty horrified by the lack of respect in his responses.

Feeling hopeless, I had been silently begging, "Where is my love, God?"

Then I heard it: "He's here."

The voice was clear. I heard it perfectly as though it was being spoken aloud into my ear, and I knew it wasn't a figment of my imagination.

I was overjoyed to receive an answer! Excited to think he was so close. I thought it meant that the time was here for my 'One' to enter my life, and he must be on the Gold Coast now.

Little did I know and I would *never* have guessed, the voice meant *literally.* He is here. Now. In my *backyard.*

Obviously, for Jackson and me to have the kind of friendship where he would help me formulate SMS

messages to my current lover, we were completely in the friend zone with each other.

A few weeks before he and his girlfriend had stayed overnight at my house when I'd put a party on for his birthday. They were living at the opposite end of the coast, so they crashed at mine for the night. I honestly thought nothing of it.

They had broken up not long after the party, and as he'd done previously under similar circumstances, Jackson had come to stay in my spare room until he found a new place to live.

We didn't sleep together while he was staying with me this time, as I was on my quest for **big love** and didn't want to dilute my energetic intention with meaningless sex.

A few weeks later, Jacko moved out of mine and in with an old friend of his, just around the corner from Jonathan and me.

I had just gotten my old job back and had two beautiful, sweet 18-

year-old girls that I'd known for years, babysitting Jonathan on the nights I had to work. They were so engaging and fun with Jonathan; he loved when they looked after him.

The first hour and a half of work went to just paying for the girls to mind Jonathan, so my finances were better than when I wasn't working, but it was still tight.

One weekend Jonathan, Jackson and his daughters - Joslyn and Sophie - and I were out on our usual alternate weekend adventure.

Jonathan's favourite people in the world are his older sisters, and vice versa. Throughout the years we'd always made an effort for the kids to be able to spend as much time with each other as possible.

That weekend, we had just been to an amazing park with a flying fox, and were just stopping off for lunch at a local pub that had a play area for the kids, when I received a message from Ruby, Jonathan's babysitter for the night.

Hi Jules. I'm so sorry, I'm really, really sick. I won't be able to watch Jonathan tonight. I'm so sorry again.

My chest constricted immediately in panic. I had to be at work in a few hours and I knew Melissa, my other babysitter, wasn't available.

"I'll watch him tonight," Jacko said, simply.

I could have kissed him, so relieved was I that he had immediately eradicated my stress.

Over the past few months Jacko had begun to change, to want something different for himself. He was maturing and growing, tired of the craziness of his lifestyle and friends.

After that weekend, he offered to watch Jonathan for each of the three nights that I worked so he could spend some time with his son and help me out. He'd always lived too far away physically and mentally for it to have been possible before.

My teenage babysitters had become a little less reliable, understandably wanting Friday and Saturday nights – the nights I needed them the most - off to go and enjoy being 18, so it seemed like a perfect solution. It saved me precious dollars, too. For

Jacko to be at the place where he didn't need to keep his weekends free for partying, and instead was prioritising being with his son and helping me out was an enormous, almost unbelievable shift.

As I finished work late in the evening, Jacko often stayed over on those nights. Most nights, both he and Jonathan were passed out asleep when I got home.

It was within this arrangement that both our hearts really opened to each other. For the first time, he was making the kinds of choices I found attractive - and he would say the same of me.

It was a miracle. We were like totally new people having a completely different experience of each other. I was no longer 'The Ice

Queen', as he saw me before, and he wasn't 'Wacko Jacko'.

These new people really liked each other, and no-one was more surprised than we were when we realised we actually tentatively, could-this-really-be- happeningly, falling in love.

Flash forward to the present and we are finally a real family, in every sense of the word: energetically, emotionally, physically and spiritually. Jackson and I are engaged to be married, raising our son together, and I am pregnant with our second child, our daughter. We are happy, I've never felt so loved and cared for. We are now each other's safe haven.

After so many years of stumbling in the dark, I honestly feel it was my commitment to my heart and those five steps I took in pursuit of *real love* that seemingly propelled me to a parallel universe, where it became the most natural thing in the world to have it with the most fitting person.

May this book do the same for you, bravehearts.

Epilogue

The Dream

I had the strangest, most vivid dream upon completion of this manuscript.

In the dream, I was at home, though my home was grander than the one I currently live in, and it had a large pool and entertaining area outside.

Jackson and a few of his mates were sitting around the pool, when Greg came by to drop off some belongings of mine that I had left with him.

Greg had brought his young blonde girlfriend with

him. She and I made small talk and then I went inside the house to escape the awkwardness.

Suddenly, there was noise. I rushed out to the backyard to see Jackson with blood dripping down his face and Greg with a swollen eye.

Greg had instigated an argument with Jackson and the two had gotten into a 'blue', as they say here in Australia, throwing punches at each other.

I rushed to Jacko. My total concern was only for him and his welfare. Both men were a bit dented but fine, and, in the way guys do here in Australia, were ready to drop the whole issue and put it behind them.

Greg started packing up and made to leave. Jackson and I walked him out, our arms wrapped around each other's waists. As he drove off, Greg's face was a grimace of pain, which he was trying desperately to mask. I pitied him in that moment - nothing more.

For me, the dream brings me full circle to healing and is confirmation that I've left the past behind, gathered all the wisdom from the experience and now give my heart truly and fully to Jackson. In the dream, when I believed the experience was real, I thought to myself, "I have to put this in the book.". If that's not more evidence that **dreams come true,** I don't know what is.

Reflection

I've just discovered that we are having a little girl.

I dreamt of my children years before I first fell pregnant. In my sleep I was a mother long before I was one in waking reality.

In my dreams, my firstborn was a brown-haired boy, and the youngest a girl with blonde curls. My son does have darker hair like his father, though we are yet to see our daughter's colouring...

I could never see the face of their father though. I believe that I had to go through the process of discovery, of learning to love myself and hear my heart and intuition as a way of preserving love once I'd found it.

As I reflect on the journey that has led me to this place where I finally feel my life mirrors my heart's truest desires, I am looking for a pattern, or a final gift of wisdom that I can share with you to help you have the life of your heart and dreams.

Really, what seems most obvious to me is that the universe or God was preparing my perfect life for me long before I even knew what that would look like, and long before I was emotionally and intellectually able to receive it.

The twists and turns that seemed to take me furthest away from the path were actually still on that yellow

brick road to home.

The darkest moments were what forced the light to the surface.

So *trust*, beloveds. Listen.
Feel into your truth. Be brave.

Imagine you are blindfolded, taking God's hand. You are being led to the highest love, but it is still up to you to pick up your feet and listen to the guidance about which way to turn.

You can't fail at this, the road only leads to one place. Whether you get to your dreams quickly, or in the next life - only that is in your hands. Godspeed.

Acknowledgments

This book is my love-song to God, to my family, to my people and to those who have inspired me along the way.

Jonathan, Baby girl, Jacko, Jen, Tiana, Joz, Soph, my family, my everyday people, my reason for being, I love you all.

Mum and Dad, I know you've been with me, whispering encouragement the whole way. Thank you for your ever-present love and support.

Renee, soul sister, my truth teller, thank you. You don't know what your friendship means to me, nor the sanity and inspiration I derive from it.

Kel, you make the frontline fun. Thankyou baby for your support and love.

Christie-Marie, Alison and Marisa, your wisdom changed me and my life, the world is literally a better place for your being here. Thank you for being the gifts and lights that you are to the world.

My beautiful cover design is thanks to www.selfpubbookcovers.com/VISIONS. They were so easy to work with and I love the result. I'll definitely go back for future covers.

Jeff Brown and the 'Write Your Way Home 2016' alumni. I had just begun writing this book when I signed up for Jeff's course. I was hoping it would help me bring truth and authenticity to my writing. Jeff's writing is soul song and I was hoping my own music would pour onto the pages of this.

I learned the best authors, as with all the best musicians, take years to perfect their craft. This, my first actualisation of my life-long dream piece, is a recorder composition. I'm hoping for flute in the next and ultimately a harp song. It is, however, as near as I could get, at this time, to putting my truest heart, soul and mind and pressing it to the page like a flower. I'm hoping you can see what it may have looked like on the plant.

58883693R00064

Made in the USA
Columbia, SC
26 May 2019